INDIAN · CUISINE

Tandoori

INDIAN * CUISINE

* Tandoori *

Tiger Books International

London

© **Lustre Press Pvt. Ltd. 1996**

This edition published in 1996 by:
Tiger Books International PLC, Twickenham

ISBN: 1-85501-811-X

Recipes by:
Geeta Mathur

Project Coordinator:
Arti Arora

Production:
N.K. Nigam, Gautam Dey, Abhijeet Raha

Conceived & Designed by:
Pramod Kapoor
at
Roli Books CAD Centre

Photographer:
Dheeraj Paul

Cover photograph by:
Hemant Mehta

Printed and bound by:
Star Standard Industries Pte. Ltd., Singapore

CONTENTS

——— * ———

Kadhai (Wok) ▲

Belan (Rolling pin) - **Chakla** (Flour board) ▲

Tawa (Griddle) ►

Chimta (Tongs) ►

Kaddoo kas (Grater) ▼

Masaaldaan ► (Spice container)

Hamam dasta (Mortar pestle) ▼

Handi (Heavy-bottomed pot) ▼

Karchi (Ladles) ►

Pateela (Deep pot) ▼

TO GET YOU ACQUAINTED........

Tandoori is India's best known export, a cuisine that suits the international palate comfortably, since it is largely meat-based, lightly spiced, and easy to both cook and serve. So named because the food is cooked in a *tandoor* (large coal-fired oven), it is easily adaptable to the oven, the electrical grill or the microwave. Tandoori is akin to the western barbecue, but with more delicate flavours and with marinades which enhance the flavour of the principle ingredient. The process of cooking is fast and efficient, and it is only the preparation that may take a while. Tandoori food may be served as starters, or may form a part of the main course, eaten with the paper-thin *roomali roti*, and mint chutney.

Indian cuisine has a range and variety that is almost extraordinary, with each region contributing its own flavour. Modern Indian cooking borrows selectively from these diverse styles, assimilates and adapts them to suit the palate. The richness of Indian food, therefore continues to grow.

Regional differences in food are often so great that they make for entirely different cuisines. Perhaps, what is common are the raw ingredients, the vegetables and meats, and the spices. But, while the greater part of India is vegetarian, there are other regions where meat and chicken are considered an essential part of the daily meal. In Bengal, fish is an obsession and is referred to as *jal toru*, an underwater vegetable.

Indian food is usually eaten without starters, soups or courses, though in restaurants it is presented in this manner for less familiar diners. The main meal is eaten with either rice or *roti*, and includes at least one lentil curry called *daal*, a selection of vegetarian servings, a meat, chicken or fish fry, a sampling of chutneys and pickles, and *dahi* (yoghurt). *Papads* are served with meals, that may be sometimes accompanied by *lassi* (buttermilk)- which helps to induce sleep on a warm afternoon! Desserts are not standard. Sweets, of course, are served with almost any Indian meal, and may take the form of a South Indian *halwa*, a delicate Lucknavi *kheer* or light Bengali sweets. But, depending on the region, these may be served after, during or before an Indian meal. No wonder Indian food continues to surprise its serving and style almost as variable as its thousands of recipes.

Tej patta (Bay leaves)   **Methi dana** (Fenugreek seed)   **Khus khus** (Poppy seeds)   **Ajwain** (Carom seeds)   **Javitri** (Mace)

Raee (Mustard seeds)   **Haldi** (Turmeric powder)   **Choti elaichi** (Green cardamom)   **Heeng** (Asafoetida)   **Laung** (Cloves)

Bari elaichi (Black cardamom)   **Amchur** (Green mango powder)   **Laal mirch** (Red chilli)   **Dhania** (Coriander) *powder*   **Kaali mirch** (Black peppercorn)

SPICES — THE SWEET & SOUR OF INDIAN FOOD

The secret of Indian cuisine lies in its spices. Used lightly but in exciting combinations, they can leave the palate tingling for more, without actually taking a toll on one's digestion.

As the story goes, the West had discovered and traded with pockets of the Indian subcontinent, primarily for its rich spices.

Although, the beneficial uses of spices have been recorded in ancient treatises, but the usage has known to vary from region to region. Apart from making food palatable, spices also have inherent 'cooling' and 'warming' properties. They are added to the foods intended for pregnant women, for invalids, for the old and of course for the very young, to aid recovery or to impart stamina.

The basic Indian spices alongwith salt, are *jeera* (**cumin**) to impart fragrance to food, *haldi* (*turmeric*) to give colour and *laal mirch* (**red chilli**) to spice up the food. *Amchur* (*dry mango powder*) adds piquancy and a mere pinch of *heeng* (**asafoetida**) adds a unique taste and also aids digestion. Fresh **coriander** is the most common garnish and also adds a light fragrance.

Since fruits are seen as energy-giving, **dried fruits** are used extensively in India. Parts of fruits, berries or vegetables are dried and stored, as condiments. Several seeds too are used, each with a marked taste.

Saunf (**fennel**) is added to desserts and some vegetarian dishes to act as a flavouring agent. *Methidana* (**fenugreek seeds**) gives a touch of bitterness, *kalonji* (**onion seeds**) is used in 'heavier' cooking or for pickles. *Raee* (**mustard seeds**) adds sourness to food while *khus-khus* (**poppy seeds**) enhances the flavour of meat. Fresh *imli* (**tamarind**) imparts a sour taste and *kesar* (**saffron**), India's most expensive herb, imparts a fine fragrance alongwith a rich yellow colour.

That Indian spices can be used almost in any fashion and to enhance any taste, is obvious from the fact that Indian tea too uses spices!! *Elaichi* (**cardamom**) is added to tea for flavouring, while saffron and almonds are added to *kahwa* (Kashmiri tea).

BASIC INDIAN RECIPES

Coconut chutney

Garam Masala

Ginger-garlic paste

Green chilli paste

Coconut chutney: Grated **coconut** (160 gms), roasted **gram** (15 gms), **curry leaves** (8), **green chillies,** chopped (5), **ginger,** chopped (15 gms), **lentils (*urad daal*),** (5 gms), **mustard seeds** (5 gms), **oil** (15 ml) and **salt** (to taste). Grind coconut, green chillies, ginger and gram to a paste. Sauté mustard seeds, lentils and curry leaves. Stir in the ground paste, cook for 3-5 minutes. Allow to cool, refrigerate and use when required.

Garam masala (for 445 gms): Finely grind the following ingredients and store: **cumin seeds** (90 gms), **black pepper corns** (70 gms), **black cardamom seeds** (75 gms), **fennel seeds** (30 gms), **green cardamoms** (40 gms), **coriander seeds** (30 gms), **cloves** (20 gms), **cinnamon sticks** (20 x 2.5 cm), **mace powder** (20 gms), **black cumin seeds** (20 gms), **dry rose petals** (15 gms), **bay leaves** (15 gms), **ginger powder** (15 gms).

Ginger paste or **Garlic paste:** Soak **ginger / garlic cloves** (300 gms) overnight to soften the skin. Peel and chop roughly. Process until pulped. The pulp can be stored in an airtight container and refrigerated for 4-6 weeks.

Green Chilli paste: Take required quantity of **green chillies**, chop roughly and process until pulped.

Khoya: Boil **milk** (2 lts) in a *kadhai* (wok). Simmer till quantity is reduced to half, stirring occasionally. Continue cooking, now stirring constantly and scraping from the sides, till a thick paste-like consistency is obtained (1-1½ hrs.). Allow to cool.

Mint Chutney: Mint leaves (60 gms), **coriander leaves** (120 gms), **cumin seeds** (5 gms), **garlic cloves** (2), **green chilli** (1), **raw mango** (30 gms), **tomatoes** (45 gms), **salt** (to taste). Chop all ingredients, blend until paste-like. Refrigerate in an airtight container.

Onion paste: Peel and chop the **onions** (500 gms) in quarters. Process until pulped. Refrigerate in an airtight container for 4-6 weeks. For **Browned Onion Paste**, slice and fry the onions in a little oil, allow to cool before processing.

Paneer (Cottage Cheese): In a pot, put **milk** (3 lts) to boil. Just before it boils, add (90 ml/6 tbs) **lemon juice / vinegar** to curdle the milk. Strain the curdled milk through a muslin cloth, to allow all whey and moisture to drain. Still wrapped in the muslin, place **paneer** under a weight for 2-3 hours to allow to set into a block which can be cut or grated.

Kho

Mint Chu

Oni past

Pan

CHICKEN

Stuffed Tandoori Drumsticks (recipe on following page) ▶

Stuffed Tandoori Drumsticks

Serves: 4   Preparation time:1 hour   Cooking time: 15 minutes

Ingredients:

Chicken drumsticks 8
White pepper .... *5 gms / 1 tsp*
Salt to taste
Ginger paste(page 10) .... *5 gms / 1 tsp*
Garlic paste(page 10) .... *5 gms / 1 tsp*

For the filling:

Cottage cheese (*paneer) .... *150 gms / ¾ cup*
Green chillies, finely chopped 4
Green coriander, chopped .... *15 gms / 1 tbs*

Cumin (*jeera*) powder .... *5 gms / 1 tsp*
Yellow chilli powder .... *3 gms / ½ tsp*
Cashewnuts, finely chopped.... *15 gms / 1 tbs*

For the coating:

Cream .... *30 gms / 2 tbs*
Cheese, grated .... *15 gms / 1 tbs*
Cornflour................................... *15 gms / 1 tbs*
Butter for basting

Method:

     * For recipe of *paneer*, turn to page 10

1. Make an incision along the bottom half of the drumstick, taking care, to not cut through the other side. Carefully open the flap for the filling.

2. Mix white pepper, salt, ginger and garlic pastes together and rub into the drumsticks evenly. Keep aside for 30 minutes.

3. **For the filling**, mash cottage cheese in a bowl. Add green chillies, coriander, cumin, chilli powder, cashewnuts and salt, mix well.

4. Put one portion of filling into the flap of the marinated drumstick without overstuffing it. Secure the flap with a toothpick. Similarly, prepare all the drumsticks and refrigerate for 15 minutes.

5. **For the coating**, whisk together, the cream, cheese and cornflour in a bowl to make a smooth paste. Coat each drumstick evenly with this paste.

6. Preheat oven/tandoor/grill to 175 °C (350 °F).

7. Skewer the drumsticks and roast for 8-10 minutes, basting occasionally with butter.

8. Remove skewers from oven/tandoor/grill and hang for 3-4 minutes to let excess liquids drip. Roast again for 3-4 minutes till golden in colour.

9. Serve hot, accompanied by Mint Chutney (page 10) and salad.

◀ *Picture on preceding page*

Stir-Fried Chicken Delight

Serves: 6   Preparation time: 2½ hours   Cooking time: 45 minutes

Ingredients:

Chicken (cut into 8 pieces) .... *1 kg*	Salt to taste
Yoghurt .... *45 gms / 3 tbs*	Garam masala (page 10) .... *15 gms / 1 tbs*
Onions, chopped .... *250 gms / 1¼ cup*	Oil .... *45 ml / 3 tbs*
Ginger, ground .... *15 gms / 1 tbs*	Green coriander, chopped .... *30 gms / 2 tbs*

Method:

1. Clean and dry the chicken. Mix together, the yoghurt, onions, ground ginger, salt and garam masala well. Marinate chicken in this mixture for 2 hours.

2. Heat oil in flat, heavy bottomed vessel. Add to it, the marinated chicken alongwith excess marinade.

3. Cook on high heat for 10 minutes, stirring regularly. Lower heat and cook further, till done. Serve hot, garnished with chopped coriander.

Chilli Honey Chicken Tikka

Serves: 5   Preparation time: 3 hours 45 minutes   Cooking time: 20 minutes

Ingredients:

Chicken breast, cleaned, deboned .... *1 kg*	White pepper powder .... *3 gms / ½ tsp*
Lemon juice .... *120 ml / ½ cup*	Nutmeg (*jaiphal*) powder .... *3 gms / ½ tsp*
Honey .... *100 ml / ½ cup*	Red food colour .... *a pinch*
Red chilli powder .... *15 gms / 1 tbs*	Salt to taste
Garlic paste (page 10) .... *5 gms / 1 tsp*	Mustard oil (preferably) .... *30 gms / 2 tbs*

Method:

1. Clean and debone the chicken breast, cut into 2 inch strips.

2. Combine all ingredients (except mustard oil) in a large bowl, coat chicken strips evenly and leave to marinate for 3 hours.

3. Skewer chicken strips 2 cms apart, grill/bake/roast in a charcoal grill/oven/tandoor for 8-10 minutes, basting occasionally with mustard oil. Serve hot, garnished with onion rings and tomato slices.

Chicken Tikka

Serves: 3-4   Preparation time: 6½ hours   Cooking time: 10 minutes

Ingredients:

Chicken breasts, cut into boneless cubes *4*
Yoghurt .... *150 ml / ¾ cup*
Garlic paste (page 10) .... *5 gms / 1 tsp*
Ginger, finely chopped .... *8 gms / 1½ tsp*
Onion (small), grated *1*

Red chilli powder .... *8 gms / 1½ tsp*
Coriander powder .... *15 gms / 1 tbs*
Salt to taste
Butter for basting

Method:

1. Combine yoghurt, garlic paste, ginger, onion, chilli powder, coriander and salt together in a bowl and mix well. Add chicken cubes to the marinade and coat evenly. Cover the bowl and refrigerate for at least 6 hours or overnight.
2. Skewer the chicken cubes, roast in a preheated grill/tandoor, turning them occasionally for 8-10 minutes or until cooked through, basting at least once.
3. Remove kababs from skewers and place on a warmed serving dish. Garnish with onion rings, tomato slices and coriander leaves. Serve at once, accompanied by Mint Chutney (page 10).

Chicken and Potato Vol-au-vent

Serves: 4   Preparation time: 15-20 minutes   Cooking time: 3-4 minutes

Ingredients:

Chicken, shredded .... *50 gms*
Oil .... *15 ml / 1 tbs*
Potato, boiled, finely chopped *1*
Tomato, chopped *1*

Tabasco/Capsico sauce .... *2 gms / ½ tsp*
Salt to taste
Orange/Red food colour .... *a drop*
Vol-au-vent 8

Method:

     * Puff pastry—easily available at any bakery.

1. Heat oil, sauté chicken alongwith finely chopped potato and tomato pieces.
2. Add a dash of Tabasco/Capsico sauce, salt and orange/red colour, stir well. Remove from fire and keep aside to cool.
3. Fill the Vol-au-vent with the chicken filling, bake in a preheated oven (150 °C/300 °F) for 3-4 minutes. Serve hot.

◀ *Chicken Tikka*

Cottage Cheese Chicken Tikka

Serves: 4-6   Preparation time: 4 hours   Cooking time: 15 minutes

Ingredients:

Chicken breasts, cut into boneless cubes *1 kg*
Lemon juice .... *15 gms / 1 tbs*
Garlic paste (page 10) .... *45 gms / 3 tbs*
Salt to taste
Cottage cheese (*paneer*), grated .... *150 gms*

Cream .... *60 ml / 4 tbs*
Cornflour .... *22 gms / 1½ tbs*
Green chilli paste (page 10) ..... *10 gms / 2 tsp*
White pepper .... *6 gms / 1 tsp*
Green coriander, chopped .... *15 gms / 1 tbs*

Method:

* For recipe of *paneer*, turn to page 10.

1. Marinate chicken with lemon juice, garlic paste and salt for 1 hour

2. Mix grated cottage cheese, cream, cornflour, chilli paste, white pepper and coriander in a bowl and whisk till smooth. Marinate chicken in this mixture for at least 3 hours.

3. Skewer chicken 2 cms apart and roast in a preheated (175 °C / 350 °F) oven/tandoor/grill for 8-10 minutes. Baste with butter and roast for another 3 minutes or until golden in colour. Serve hot, garnished with tomato, onion and cucumber slices and accompanied by Mint Chutney (page 10).

Colourful Chicken Seekh Kabab

Serves: 4-5   Preparation time: 20 minutes   Cooking time: 8-10 minutes

Ingredients:

Chicken, minced .... *800 gms*
Eggs, whisked *2*
Cumin (*jeera*) powder .... *10 gms / 2 tsp*
Yellow chilli powder .... *5 gms / 1 tsp*
White pepper powder .... *5 gms / 1 tsp*
Salt to taste
Oil .... *40 ml / 2²/₃ tbs*
Cashewnut paste .... *50 gms / 3¹/₃ tbs*
Ginger, chopped .... *20 gms / 4 tsp*
Green chillies, chopped .... *15 gms / 6*
Garlic paste (page 10) .... *20 gms / 4 tsp*

Green coriander, chopped .... *15 gms / 1 tbs*
Onions, finely chopped .... *10 gms / 2 tsp*
Cottage cheese (*paneer*), grated
.... *50gms/¼cup*
Garam masala (page 10) .... *5 gms / 1 tsp*
Capsicum, finely chopped .... *10 gms / 2 tsp*
Tomatoes, finely chopped .... *10 gms / 2 tsp*
Butter for basting .... *50 gms / 3¹/₃ tbs*
Chaat masala .... *5 gms / 1 tsp*
Lemon juice .... *30 ml / 2 tbs*

Method:

1. To the minced chicken, add eggs, cumin powder, yellow chilli powder, white pepper, salt and oil. Mix well and keep aside for 15 minutes.
2. Mix in the cashewnut paste, ginger, chillies, garlic paste, green coriander, onions, cottage cheese and garam masala. Divide into 8 equal portions and shape into balls. Skewer the balls, moisten hands and spread the balls by pressing each along the length of the skewers to make 10 cm long kababs, 4 cm apart.
3. Mix capsicum and tomato, gently press over kababs evenly from top to bottom.
4. Roast in a preheated (175 ºC / 350 ºF) oven for 8-10 minutes or until golden brown, basting occassionally with butter.
5. Sprinkle chaat masala and lemon juice. Serve hot, garnished with onion rings and lemon wedges.

Creamy Chicken Tikka

Serves: 4-6   Preparation time: 3 hours 45 minutes   Cooking time: 12 minutes

Ingredients:

Chicken breast, cut into boneless cubes *1 kg*
Garlic paste (page 10) .... *30 gms / 2 tbs*
Ginger paste (page 10) .... *30 gms / 2 tbs*
Salt to taste
White pepper powder .... *5 gms / 1 tsp*
Egg, whisked *1*
Cheddar cheese, grated .... *60 gms / 4 tbs*

Green chillies, deseeded, finely chopped *8*
Green coriander,
finely chopped .... 20 gms / 4 tsp
Mace and Nutmeg powder .... *3 gms / ½ tsp*
Cornflour .... *10 gms / 2 tsp*
Cream .... *160 ml / ²/₃ cup*
Oil/Butter for basting

Method:

1. Rub garlic-ginger pastes, salt and white pepper into the chicken cubes, keep aside for 15 minutes.
2. To the whisked egg, add cheese, green chillies, coriander, mace-nutmeg powder, cornflour and cream. Mix well and coat the chicken cubes with prepared mixture. Marinate for at least 3 hours.
3. Skewer the chicken cubes 2 cms apart and roast in a preheated (137 °C / 275 °F) oven/ grill/tandoor for 5-8 minutes. Hang skewers for 3-5 minutes to let excess liquid drip, brush with oil and roast again for 3 minutes.
4. Serve at once, garnished with chopped coriander, tomato slices and lemon wedges, accompanied by Mint Chutney (page 10).

◀ *Creamy Chicken Tikka*

Tandoori Chicken

Serves:4-5   Preparation time: 3½ hours   Cooking time: 15-20 minutes

Ingredients:

Chicken, whole, skinned (600 gms each) *2*
Salt to taste
Red chilli powder .... *5 gms / 1 tsp*
Lemon juice .... *45 gms / 3 tbs*
Yoghurt .... *100 gms / ½ cup*
Cream .... *100 gms / ½ cup*
Garlic paste (page 10) .... *12 gms / 2½ tsp*

Ginger paste (page 10) .... *12 gms / 2½ tsp*
Cumin (*jeera*) powder .... *5 gms / 1 tsp*
Garam masala (page 10) .... *3 gms / ½ tsp*
Saffron (*kesar*) .... *a pinch*
Orange colour ....*a drop*
Oil/Butter for basting
Chaat masala .... *5 gms / 1 tsp*

Method:

1. Clean chicken, make deep incisions on the breast, thighs and legs of the chicken.

2. Combine together, the salt, red chillies and lemon juice to make a paste. Rub this paste into the chicken evenly. Set aside for half an hour.

3. In a bowl, whisk yoghurt, cream and remaining ingredients to make a smooth paste.

4. Coat the chicken evenly with this mixture. Keep aside for 2½-3 hours.

5. Skewer the chicken leaving a gap of 3-4 inches between each. Roast in a moderately hot tandoor/charcoal grill or a preheated oven (175 °C / 350 °F) for 8-10 minutes. Remove, baste with butter/oil and roast for another 3-4 minutes.

6. Cut into pieces, sprinkle chaat masala and serve hot, garnished with onion rings and lemon wedges.

Batter-coated Chicken Kabab

Serves: 4   Preparation time: 2½ hours   Cooking time: 10 minutes

Ingredients:

Chicken breast, cleaned
and cut into four *6*
Ginger paste (page 10) .... *30 gms / 2 tbs*
Garlic paste (page 10) .... *30 gms / 2 tbs*
Lemon juice .... *30 gms / 2 tbs*
White pepper powder .... *5 gms / 1 tsp*

Salt to taste
Butter.. *45 gms / 3 tbs*
Oil .... *10 ml / 2 tsp*
Gramflour (*besan*) .... *45 gms / 3 tbs*
Ginger, chopped .... *30 gms / 2 tbs*
Green coriander, chopped ..... *30 gms / ½ cup*

◀ *Tandoori Chicken*

Bread crumbs, pounded .... *60 gms / ½ cup*
Green cardamom (*choti elaichi*), pounded
.... *3 gms / ½ tbs*

Eggs(yolks only) *2*
Cumin (*jeera*) seeds .... *5 gms/1 tsp*
Saffron (*kesar*) .... *a pinch*

Method:

1. Rub ginger and garlic pastes, lemon juice, white pepper and salt into the chicken pieces and keep aside for at least 1 hour.

2. Heat butter and oil in a *kadhai* (wok), brown the gramflour (2 tbs), add chopped ginger, coriander, bread crumbs and the marinated chicken. Stir for 5 minutes.

3. **For the batter**, whisk the egg yolks, cumin powder, remaining gramflour and saffron.

4. Coat each chicken piece with the egg batter and skewer the pieces close together.

5. Roast in a preheated (175 °C / 350 °F) oven/charcoal grill/tandoor till cooked to a golden colour. Sprinkle cardamom powder and serve hot.

Ginger Chicken Kababs

Serves:4   Preparation time: 1½ hours   Cooking time: 15 minutes

Ingredients:

Chicken breasts, cut into boneless cubes *1kg*
Green chilli paste (page 10) ..... *15 gms / 1 tbs*
White pepper .... *10 gms / 2 tsp*
Salt to taste
Ginger paste (page 10) .... *60 gms / 4 tbs*

Malt vinegar .... *20 ml / 4 tsp*
Yoghurt, drained .... *200 gms / 1 cup*
Cream .... *60 gms / 4 tbs*
Butter for basting

Method:

1. Clean the chicken cubes. Mix green chilli paste, white pepper, salt, ginger paste and vinegar in a large bowl, rub into the chicken cubes. Keep aside for 30 minutes.

2. Mix yoghurt with cream in a seperate bowl. Add the chicken cubes to the mixture and keep aside for ½ hour.

3. Skewer chicken cubes and roast in a preheated (175 °C / 350 °F) oven/tandoor/grill for 5-8 minutes. Hang skewers to allow excess liquids to drip. Roast again for 4-5 minutes. Remove from skewers.

4. Serve hot, garnished with julienned ginger, accompanied by Mint Chutney (page 10).

◀ *Ginger Chicken Kababs*

Chicken Seekh Kabab

Serves: 4   Preparation time: 45 minutes   Cooking time: 8-10 minutes

Ingredients:

Chicken, minced .... *1 kg*
Eggs *2*
Cumin (*jeera*) powder .... *10 gms / 2 tsp*
Garam masala(page 10) .... *10 gms / 2 tsp*
Red chilli powder .... *7 gms / 1½ tsp*
White pepper .... *5 gms / 1 tsp*

Salt to taste
Oil .... 15 ml / 1tbs + for basting
Ginger, finely chopped .... *45 gms / 3 tbs*
Onions, finely chopped .... *30 gms / 2 tbs*
Cashewnuts, finely pounded *50 gms / ¼ cup*
Green coriander, chopped .... *30 gms / 2 tbs*

Method:

1. Whisk egg in a bowl. Add cumin powder, garam masala, chillies, white pepper, salt and oil to the mince, mix well and set aside for 30 minutes.

2. Add ginger, onions and cashewnuts, mix well.

3. Preheat oven to 150 °C (300 °F).

4. Divide prepared mince into 8 equal portions. Wrap each portion along the length of the skewer, making each kabab about 4 to 5 inches long and 2 inches apart.

5. Roast in a hot tandoor for 5-6 minutes, baste with oil just once and roast again till light golden brown in colour.

6. Serve hot, garnished with onion rings, tomato slices and lemon wedges, accompanied by Mint Chutney (page 10).

Grilled Chicken Strips

Serves: 3-4   Preparation time: 6 hours   Cooking time: 30 minutes

Ingredients:

Chicken breasts, (2" × 1") strips .... *1 kg*
For the marinade:
Vinegar .... *45 gms / 3 tbs*
Onion (medium), finely chopped *1*
Ginger, finely chopped .... *10 gms / 2 tsp*
Garlic, finely chopped .... *10 gms / 2 tsp*
Cumin (*jeera*) powder .... *30 gms / 2 tbs*

Coriander powder .... *10 gms / 2 tsp*
Fennel (*saunf*) seeds .... *15 gms / 1 tbs*
Green cardamom (*choti elaichi*), ground *8*
Cinnamon (*daalchini*), ground .. *5 gms / 1 tsp*
Cloves (*laung*), whole *8*
Peppercorns *20*
Cayenne pepper (*whole dried red chillies*)

.... *3 gms / 1 tsp*   Tomato purée .... *15 gms / 1 tbs*
Salt to taste

Method:

1. Combine all ingredients for the marinade and blend to a smooth paste.
2. Place the chicken strips on a flat dish. Pour the marinade over and rub into the chicken strips. Cover and refrigerate for 4-5 hours.
3. Preheat oven to 138 °C (275 °F).
4. Line baking tray with aluminium foil and spread the chicken strips on the tray. (You will need to grill in two batches). Grill for 10 minutes, turn pieces over and grill for another 10 minutes until chicken is browned in spots. Chicken strips can also be grilled in a tandoor for 8-10 minutes, basting twice until lightly browned.
5. Remove and place on a warmed serving dish. Serve hot, accompanied by Mint Raita (page 80) and a rice dish.

Chicken Soya Kababs

Serves: 4-5   Preparation time: 45 minutes   Cooking time: 8-10 minutes

Ingredients:

Chicken breasts, cut into boneless cubes *4*
Lemon juice .... *15 ml / 1 tbs*
Black pepper powder .... *7 gms / 1½ tsp*
Garlic paste (page 10) .... *10 gms / 2 tsp*
Salt .... *5 gms / 1 tsp*
Oil .... *15 ml / 1 tbs*
Soya sauce .... *30 gms / 2 tbs*
Butter/Oil for basting

Method:

1. Rub lemon juice into the chicken cubes and mix well. Keep aside for 30 minutes.
2. Pat the chicken cubes dry and sprinkle black pepper powder.
3. Mix garlic paste, salt, oil and soya sauce, add the chicken cubes and coat well. Marinate for 2-3 hours.
4. Preheat oven to 175 °C (350 °F). Thread chicken on to the skewers, 2 cms apart. Roast for 8-10 minutes or until cooked through basting just once.
5. Serve hot, accompanied by Chilli sauce.

LAMB

Tangy Mint Lamb Chops (recipe on following page) ▶

Tangy Mint Lamb Chops

Serves: 4-5   Preparation time: 4 hours   Cooking time:12-15 minutes

Ingredients:

Lamb chops, cleaned .... *1 kg*
Cumin (*jeera*) powder .... *5 gms / 1 tsp*
White pepper powder .... *15 gms /1 tbs*
Garam masala (page 10) .... *10 gms / 2 tsp*
Lemon juice .... *25 ml / 5 tsp*
Cream .... *60 ml / 4 tbs*
Yoghurt, drained .... *150 gms / ¾ cup*
Mint /Coriander
chutney (page 10) .... *250 gms / 1¼ cup*

Cornflour .... *30 gms / 2 tbs*
Papaya paste (optional) .... *45 gms / 3 tbs*
Garlic paste (page 10) .... *15 gms / 1 tbs*
Ginger paste (page 10) .... *15 gms /1 tbs*
Fenugreek (*kasoori methi*)
powder .... *5 gms /1 tsp*
Oil for basting
Salt to taste

Method:

1. Mix cumin powder, white pepper, garam masala, lemon juice and salt. Add the lamb chops and marinate for 1 hour.
2. Mix cream, yoghurt, fresh mint/coriander chutney and cornflour. Add remaining ingredients and whisk to a fine paste. Add to the lamb chops and marinate for another 2½ to 3 hours.
3. Skewer lamb chops 2 cms apart and roast in a preheated (175 °C / 350°F) oven tandoor/ charcoal grill for 8-10 minutes. Hang skewers for a few minutes to allow excess marinade to drip. Baste with oil and roast for another 4-5 minutes.
4. Sprinkle lemon juice, garnish with slices of cucumber, tomato and onion, serve hot.

Mughlai Lamb Chops

Serves: 4-6   Preparation time: 3-4 hours   Cooking time: 20 minutes

Ingredients:

Lamb chops, cleaned and flattened .... *1 kg*
Papaya paste .... *60 gms / 4 tbs*
Ginger paste (page 10) ....*50 gms / 3 ¹/₃tbs*
Garlic paste (page 10) .... *45 gms / 3 tbs*
Black pepper powder .... *5 gms / 1 tsp*
Salt to taste

Yoghurt, drained .... *80 gms / 5 ¹/₃ cup*
Green cardamoms (*choti elaichi*),
pounded .... *10 gms / 2 tsp*
Garam masala (page 10) .... *20 gms / 4 tsp*
Lemon juice .... *40 gms / 2 ²/₃tbs*
Orange colour .... *a pinch*

◀ *Tangy Mint Lamb Chops (picture on preceding page)*

Method:

1. To the lamb chops, add papaya paste, ginger and garlic pastes, black pepper powder and salt, mix well and marinate for 2 hours.
2. Whisk yoghurt, green cardamom powder, garam masala, lemon juice and orange colour in a large bowl, coat the chops evenly with this mixture. Cover and keep aside for 1 hour.
3. Skewer chops 1" apart and roast in a preheated (175 °C / 350 °F) oven/tandoor/grill for 9-10 minutes, basting occasionally with butter.
4. Serve hot, accompanied by a salad.

Masala Lamb Steaks

Serves: 4   Preparation time: 10 minutes   Cooking time:7-10 minutes

Ingredients:

Lamb steaks (2"×2") 8
Onion, minced 1
Garlic, crushed .... *15 gms / 1 tbs*
Green chilli paste (page 10) ..... *15 gms / 1 tbs*
Poppy seeds (*khus khus*), ground .... *15 gms / 1 tbs*
Garam masala (page 10) .... *15 gms / 1 tbs*
Salt to taste

Method:

1. Mix onion, garlic and green chilli paste alongwith poppy seeds, garam masala and salt.
2. Marinate steaks in this mixture for 2 hours.
3. Roast in a charcoal grill / tandoor till cooked as desired.
4. Serve hot, garnished with onion rings and accompanied by pickled green chillies.

Pickled Lamb Chops

Serves: 4-5   Preparation time: 2½ hours   Cooking time: 30 minutes

Ingredients:

Lamb chops, each on 2 bones 8
Papaya / Meat tenderizer .... *small piece*
Ginger paste (page 10) .... *10 gms / 2 tsp*
Garlic paste (page 10) .... *10 gms / 2 tsp*
Salt to taste
Gramflour (*besan*) .... *10 gms / 2 tsp*
Yoghurt, whisked .... *50 gms / ¼ cup*
Red chilli powder .... *15 gms / 3 tsp*
Onion (*kalonji*) seeds .... *5 gms / 1 tsp*
Aniseed .... *5 gms / 1 tsp*
Black cardamom (*bari elaichi*) *2 gms / ½ tsp*
Black pepper powder .... *5 gms / 1 tsp*

Cloves (*laung*) .... *3 gms / ²/₃ tsp*	Chaat masala .... *5 gms / 1 tsp*
Mustard oil (*sarson ka tel*) ...... *50 ml / 3¹/₃ tbs*	Lemon juice .... *15 ml / 1 tbs*
Mustard (*raee*) seeds .... *5 gms / 1 tsp*	

Method:

1. Flatten the chops with a steak hammer.
2. Rub the chops with papaya, ginger-garlic pastes and salt, keep aside.
3. Roast the gramflour in a pan till light brown and sprinkle over the lamb chops.
4. To the yoghurt, add the remaining ingredients (except chaat masala and lemon juice). Mix well to a fine batter. Marinate the chops in this marinade for 2 hours.
5. Preheat the oven to 175 °C (350 °F).
6. Skewer the chops and roast in a hot tandoor or oven until cooked.
7. Remove the chops from the skewer. Sprinkle chaat masala and lemon juice, serve hot, accompanied by a green salad.

Ginger Lamb Chops

Serves: 4 Preparation time: 4 hours 30 minutes Cooking time: 20 minutes

Ingredients:

Lamb chops *12*	Cream .... *45 gms / 3 tbs*
Papaya paste .... *30 gms / 2 tbs*	Cumin (*jeera*) powder .... *15 gms / 1 tbs*
Salt to taste	Red chilli powder .... *10 gms / 2 tsp*
Ginger paste (page 10) .... *45 gms / 3 tbs*	Garam masala (page 10) .... *10 gms / 2 tsp*
Garlic paste (page 10) .... *20 gms / 4 tsp*	Lemon juice .... *30 gms / 2 tbs*
Black pepper powder .... *5 gms / 1 tsp*	Butter/Oil for basting

Method:

1. Clean chops and flatten them slightly with a spatula. Mix together, the papaya paste, salt, ginger-garlic pastes and pepper, rub it into the chops. Keep aside for 3-4 hours.
2. Whisk cream alongwith cumin powder, red chilli powder, garam masala and lemon juice. Coat the chops well and leave to marinate further for an hour.
3. Preheat oven to 175 °C (350 °F). Skewer chops an inch apart and roast in oven/tandoor/grill for 10-12 minutes.
4. Hang skewers for a couple of minutes to let excess liquids drip. Baste with butter and roast again for 3-4 minutes until lightly browned. Garnish with chopped coriander and serve hot.

◀ *Ginger Lamb Chops*

Potato-coated Lamb Chops

Serves: 4-5   Preparation time: 1½ hours   Cooking time: 30 minutes

Ingredients:

Lamb chops 12	**For the coating:**
Water .... 600 ml / 3 cups	Potatoes, boiled, peeled, mashed .... ½ kg
Onion, (medium) sliced 1	Ginger, finely chopped .... 5 gms / 1 tsp
Ginger, sliced .... 5 gms / 1 tsp	Green chillies, finely chopped 2
Garlic cloves 6	Green coriander, chopped .... 15 gms / 1 tbs
Peppercorns 6-8	Black pepper powder .... 3 gms / ½ tsp
Cinnamon (*daalchini*) stick (1 inch) 1	Red chilli powder .... 3 gms / ½ tsp
Black cardamoms (*bari elaichi*) 2	Salt to taste
Cloves (*laung*) 4	Bread crumbs, powdered
Salt to taste	

Method:

1. Put chops in a pan. Add water, sliced onions, ginger, garlic cloves, peppercorns, cinnamon, cardamom, cloves and salt. Cover the pan and let it simmer on low heat till the chops are tender. Remove chops from the stock and keep aside.

2. **For the coating**, add ginger, green chillies and coriander, black pepper powder, red chillies and salt to the potatoes. Mix well.

3. Divide potato mixture into 12 portions.

4. Moisten palm and spread one portion of the potato mixture on it. Place chop in the middle and wrap mashed potato around the chop, shaping it well. Similarly, prepare the remaining chops and keep aside.

5. Spread the powdered bread crumbs in a flat tray. Roll each drumstick in the breadcrumbs to coat evenly and keep aside.

6. Heat oil in a *kadhai* (wok) till it is smoking.

7. Fry the chops, two at a time till they are crisp and nicely browned from all sides.

8. Drain on paper napkin and serve hot, accompanied by salad and /or Mint Chutney (page 10).

◀ *Potato-coated Lamb Chops*

Raan

Serves: 4   Preparation time: 2½ hours   Cooking time: 2 hours

Ingredients:

Lamb, leg piece *1*
Brown onion paste(page 10) ... *60 gms / 4 tbs*
Garlic paste (page 10) .... *10 gms / 2 tsp*
Ginger paste (page 10) .... *10 gms / 2 tsp*
Green cardamom (*choti elaichi*) seeds,
powdered .... *3 gms / ½ tsp*
Yoghurt .... *60 gms / 4 tbs*

Red chilli powder .... *10 gms / 2 tsp*
Salt to taste
Garam masala (page 10) .... *3 gms / ½ tsp*
Black pepper powder .... *5 gms / 1 tsp*
Saffron (*kesar*) .... *a pinch*
Chaat masala
Oil for basting

Method:

1. Clean the leg of lamb and prick thoroughly down to the bone with a fork. Mix all the ingredients. Apply evenly and leave to marinate for 2 hours.

2. Place leg in a baking tray with water (2 cups). Bake in a pre-heated (175° C / 350 ° F) oven for at least one hour turning the leg twice /thrice to ensure that the leg cooks evenly. Roast till all the liquids dry up.

3. Baste with oil and grill/roast in a moderately hot tandoor till well done.

4. Sprinkle chaat masala and serve hot, garnished with onion rings and accompanied by Mint Chutney (page 10).

Meat Puffs

Serves: 4   Preparation time: 1½ hours   Cooking time: 15 minutes

Ingredients:

Lamb, minced.................................... *250 gms*
Flour .... *45 gms / 3 tbs*
Baking powder........................... *2 gms / ¼ tsp*
Eggs, whisked *3*
Green chillies, finely chopped *2*
Green coriander, chopped ....*22 gms /1 ½ tbs*

Red chilli powder .... *5 gms / 1 tsp*
Turmeric (*haldi*) powder .... *3 gms / ½ tsp*
Chaat masala .... *15 gms / 1 tbs*
Salt
Oil for frying

Method:

1. Sift flour and baking powder in a bowl, add the eggs and mix well. Gradually add enough water to make a thick creamy batter, whisking well.

2. Stir in the lamb, green chillies, coriander, chilli powder, turmeric and salt. The mixture should be like stiff porridge. Set aside to allow to ferment for 1 hour.

3. Heat oil in a frying pan till it is smoking. Drop in a few spoonfuls of meat batter at a time, lower heat and fry meat puffs on each side till crisp and brown. Drain excess oil. Sprinkle chaat masala and serve hot, accompanied by Mint Chutney (page 10) and salad.

Seekh Kabab

Serves: 4-6   Preparation time: 2 hours   Cooking time: 10 minutes

Ingredients:

Lamb, minced	½ kg	
Papaya, ground	15 gms / 1 tbs	
Ginger paste (page 10)	10 gms / 2 tsp	
Garlic paste (page 10)	10 gms / 2 tsp	
Green coriander, chopped	22 gms / 4 tsp	
Green chillies, finely chopped	3	
Red chilli powder	5 gms / 1 tsp	
Black pepper, ground	5 gms / 1 tsp	
Cinnamon (*daalchini*) powder	3 gms / ½ tsp	

Cumin (*jeera*) seeds, ground ..... 5 gms / 1 tsp
Brown onion paste (page 10) 45 gms / 3 tbs
Oil .... 15 ml / 1 tbs
Yoghurt .... 22 gms / 4 tsp
Gramflour (*besan*),
lightly roasted .... 37 gms / 2½ tbs
Nutmeg (*jaiphal*) powder .... a pinch
Mace (*javitri*) powder .... a pinch

Method:

1. Combine minced lamb and papaya paste together. Set aside for 1 hour.

2. Mix together the ginger-garlic pastes, coriander and green chillies, ground spices, brown onion paste, oil, yoghurt and gramflour into the minced lamb and knead well for 7-8 minutes. Set aside for 30 minutes.

3. Moisten hands and spread the mince mixture along the length of the skewer making each kabab 3-4" long and 1" apart.

4. Roast over a charcoal grill or in a preheated (175 °C / 350 °F) oven for 8-10 minutes. Avoid turning too often as the kababs may fall off the skewers. Baste with butter and roast till kababs are uniformly brown.

5. Serve hot, garnished with onion rings and accompanied by Mint Chutney (page 10).

Barbecued Liver

Serves: 4-6   Preparation time: 3 hours 30 minutes   Cooking time: 30 minutes

Ingredients:

Liver, cut into cubes .... 250 gms	Green coriander, chopped .... 10 gms / 2 tsp
Ginger paste (page 10) .... 15 gms /1tbs	Turmeric (haldi) powder .... 2 gms / ½ tsp
Garlic paste (page 10) .... 5 gms / 1 tsp	Carom (ajwain) seeds .... 2 gms / ½ tsp
Onion paste (page 10) .... 5 gms / 1 tsp	Dried fenugreek powder
Yoghurt .... 30 gms / 2 tbs	(kasoori methi) .... 5 gms / 1 tsp
Red chilli powder .... 3 gms / ¾ tsp	Salt to taste
Garam masala (page 10) .... 3 gms / ¾ tsp	Oil .... 15 ml / 1 tbs
Cumin (jeera) powder .... 2 gms / ½ tsp	Oil/Butter for basting

Method:

1. Rub ginger, garlic and onion pastes into the liver cubes and set aside for an hour.
2. Mix the remaining ingredients into the yoghurt and evenly coat the liver cubes. Leave to marinate for at least 2 hours.
3. Preheat oven to 150 °C / 300 °F.
4. Thread cubes gently onto the skewers. Roast/grill/bake till half done (10 minutes).
5. Drain excess liquids, baste once and roast again for 4-5 minutes till cooked through.
6. Serve at once, accompanied by salad and /or Mint Chutney (page 10).

Spiced Kidneys

Serves: 4   Preparation time: 10 minutes   Cooking time: 25-30 minutes

Ingredients:

Lamb kidneys, cut into pieces 8	Green chillies, chopped 2
Oil .... 30 ml / 2 tbs	Tomatoes (large), blanched, chopped 2
Onion (large), sliced 1	Salt to taste
Garlic, crushed .... 7 gms / 1 ½ tsp	Green pepper (large), thinly sliced 1
Ginger paste (page 10) .... 4 gms / ¾ tsp	Black pepper powder .... 3 gms / ²/₃ tsp

Method:

1. Heat oil and sauté sliced onion until golden in colour.

2. Add crushed garlic and ginger paste. Stir-fry for 2-3 minutes.

3. Then add green chillies and kidneys and stir for 4-5 mins.

4. Add chopped tomatoes and salt, lower heat, cover pan and cook on low heat till kidneys are tender and completely cooked.

5. Stir in sliced green peppers and black pepper powder.

6. Garnish with chopped coriander and serve hot.

Barbecued Lamb

Serves: 4-5   Preparation time: 3 ½ hours   Cooking time: 20 minutes

Ingredients:

Lamb leg, cut into boneless cubes .... *1 kg*
Lemon juice .... *30 gms / 2 tbs*
Green chilli paste (page 10) ..... *15 gms / 1 tbs*
Ginger paste (page 10) .... *50 gms / 3 1/3 tbs*
Garlic paste (page 10) .... *40 gms / 2 2/3 tbs*
Salt to taste

White pepper powder .... *10 gms / 2 tsp*
Cream ....*200 gms / 1 cup*
Cheese, grated .... *70 gms / 4 2/3 tbs*
Green coriander, chopped .... *30 gms / 2 tbs*
Cumin (*jeera*) powder .... *15 gms / 1 tbs*
Butter for basting

Method:

1. Make a marinade with lemon juice, green chilli paste, ginger and garlic pastes, salt and white pepper. Marinate the lamb in this marinade for 2½ hours.

2. Mix together, the cream, cheese, coriander and cumin powder. Add to this, the lamb mixture and marinate for another 1 hour.

3. Thread the lamb pieces onto the skewers, 3 cms apart.

4. Cook in a moderately hot oven (175 °C / 350 °F) / tandoor for 15 minutes or on a charcoal grill for 10-12 minutes.

5. Brush with butter and cook for another 3-4 minutes.

6. Remove from skewers and serve hot, accompanied by salad and /or Mint Chutney (page 10).

◀ *Barbecued Lamb*

Shaami Kababs

Serves: 4   Preparation time: 1 hour   Cooking time: 25-30 minutes

Ingredients:

Lamb, minced .... *500 gms*
Lentils (*chana daal*) .... *100 gms / ½ cup*
Garlic cloves *10*
Ginger, chopped .... *10 gms / 2 tsp*
Onion(medium), chopped *2*
Cumin (*jeera*) seeds .... *5 gms / 1 tsp*
Green cardamoms (*choti elaichi*) *4*
Cinnamon (*daalchini*) piece (1 inch) *1*
Cloves (*laung*) *5*
Peppercorns *8-10*
Turmeric (*haldi*) powder .... *3 gms / ½ tsp*
Salt to taste

Red chilli powder .... *5 gms / 1 tsp*
Egg *1*
For the filling:
Onions, finely chopped .... *45 gms / 3 tbs*
Mint, finely chopped .... *30 gms / 2 tbs*
Green coriander, finely chopped ....
.... *30 gms / 2 tbs*
Ginger, finely chopped .... *5 gms / 1 tsp*
Green chillies, finely chopped *4*
Chaat masala .... *5 gms / 1 tsp*
Salt to taste
Oil for frying

Method:

1. Wash lentils. Mix with garlic, ginger, onions, cumin, cardamom, cinnamon, cloves, peppercorns alongwith the mince in a *handi*(pot) and enough water to completely submerge the mince. Bring to a boil, reduce heat, cover the dish and simmer till the mince is completely dry.

2. Remove from heat, allow the mince to cool and blend to make a fine paste. Transfer paste to a flat dish, add turmeric, salt, red chilli powder and egg, mix well. Divide the mixture into 15 equal portions and shape into balls.

3. **For the filling**, mix together, the onion, mint, coriander, ginger, green chillies, chaat masala and salt. Divide equally into 15 portions

4. Flatten each mince ball on a wet palm and place one portion of filling in the centre, reshape to make a round patty.

5. Heat oil in a *kadhai* (wok) till it is smoking. Deep fry the mince patties until crisp and brown on both sides.

6. Serve hot, garnished with sliced boiled egg and accompanied by Mint Chutney (page 10).

◀ *Shammi Kabab*

Lamb Kabab with a hint of Fenugreek

Serves: 6   Preparation time: 4 hours 15 minutes   Cooking time: 15 minutes

Ingredients:

Lamb(leg), deboned and cubed ....*1 kg*	Red chilli powder .... *5 gms / 1 tsp*
Yoghurt...*150 ml / ¾ cup*	Salt to taste
Coriander powder .... *15 gms / 1 tbs*	Garlic paste (page 10) .... *30 gms / 2 tbs*
Dried fenugreek powder	Ginger paste (page10) .... *30 gms / 2 tbs*
(*kasoori methi*) .... *5 gms / 1 tsp*	Orange colour (optional) .... *a pinch*
Turmeric (*haldi*) powder .... *5 gms / 1 tsp*	Oil/Butter for basting

Method:

1. Combine yoghurt, ground coriander, dried fenugreek powder, turmeric, chilli powder, salt, garlic-ginger pastes and whisk well.

2. Pour yoghurt mixture over lamb cubes and mix to coat the cubes evenly. Baste with oil, cover the bowl and set aside for 4 hours.

3. Thread cubes on to the skewers and roast in a preheated (175 °C /350 °F) oven/grill/ tandoor for 5 to 6 minutes. Remove from heat, baste with oil and roast again for 3-4 minutes or until cooked through.

4. Serve hot, garnished with lemon wedges and accompanied by Mint Chutney (page10).

Spicy Lamb Shanks

Serves: 4-5   Preparation time: 2 hours   Cooking time: 1 hour

Ingredients:

Lamb, 10 cm shanks on the bone ....*1 kg*	Green cardamoms (*choti elaichi*) *10*
Ginger paste (page 10) ....*50 gms / 3¹/₃ tbs*	Maize flour (*makke ka atta*) .....*3 gms / ²/₃ tsp*
Bay leaves (*tej patta*) *2*	Oil .... *60 ml / 4 tbs*
Cinnamon (*daalchini*) sticks.........................*4*	Red chilli powder .... *10 gms / 2 tsp*
Garam masala .... *15 gms / 3 tsp*	Salt to taste
Garlic paste (page 10) ....*50 gms / 3¹/₃ tbs*	

Method:

1. Remove excess fat from the lamb. Prick thoroughly down to the bone with a fork to break all the fibres. The success of the dish depends upon how well this is done.

◀ *Lamb Kabab with a hint of Fenugreek*

2. Apply the ginger and garlic pastes alongwith red chilli powder, salt, maize flour and garam masala evenly over the shanks. Leave to marinate for at least 1-2 hours.

3. Heat oil in a pan, add the whole spices and sauté over medium heat till they crackle.

4. Arrange the shanks in the pan and sauté over medium heat for 10-15 minutes until the meat changes colour.

5. Add hot water (2 cups), stir and cover, leave to simmer for 40 minutes or until it is completely tender.

6. Remove each piece with a tong and keep aside.

7. Strain the sauce and simmer until it becomes a thick concentrate (about 200-50 ml).

8. Arrange the shanks in a serving platter, pour the sauce on top. Serve hot, garnished with slices of tomato and cucumber, onion rings and lemon wedges.

Mughlai Kabab

Serves: 4-5   Preparation time: 3½ hours   Cooking time: 20 minutes

Ingredients:

Lamb (leg or shoulder),
cut into boneless cubes .... *1 kg*
Ginger paste (page 10) .... *45 gms / 3 tbs*
Garlic paste (page 10) .... *45 gms / 3 tbs*
Vinegar .... *45 ml / 3 tbs*
Red chilli powder .... *10 gms / 2 tsp*
Black pepper, ground .... *5 gms / 1 tsp*
Salt to taste

Cream .... *45 gms / 3 tbs*
Cheese .... *45 gms / 3 tbs*
Garam masala (page 10) .... *5 gms / 1 tsp*
Cumin (*jeera*) powder .... *5 gms / 1 tsp*
Saffron (*kesar*) .... *a pinch*
Fenugreek powder
(*kasoori methi*) .... *3 gms / ½ tsp*
Butter for basting

Method:

1. Mix ginger, garlic, vinegar, red chilli powder, black pepper and salt together.

2. Marinate the lamb cubes in the prepared mixture for 2 hours.

3. In another bowl, mix cream, cheese, garam masala, cumin powder, saffron and fenugreek powder together. Add marinated lamb to this mixture, set aside for 1 hour.

4. Preheat oven to 175 °C (350 °F). Skewer the lamb cubes, 2 cms apart. Roast in the oven/charcoal grill/tandoor for 8-10 minutes. Hang the skewers for a few minutes to allow excess liquids to drip. Baste with butter and cook further for another 3-4 min.

5. Serve hot, garnished with chopped coriander and cream, accompanied by lemon wedges and onion rings.

◀ *Mughlai Kabab*

Lamb Kabab with whole spices

Serves: 4-5   Preparation time: 3½ hours   Cooking time: 20 minutes

Ingredients:

Lamb, cut into boneless cubes .... *1 kg*
Black pepper, crushed .... *6 gms / 1 1/3 tsp*
Butter for basting .... *50 gms / 3 1/3 tbs*
Cheese, grated .... *70 gms / 4 1/3 tbs*
Cumin (jeera) powder .... *5 gms / 1 tsp*
Garam masala (page 10) .... *15 gms / 1 tbs*
Garlic paste (page 10) .... *40 gms / 2 2/3 tbs*
Ginger paste (page 10) .... *50 gms / 3 1/3 tbs*

Oil .... *70 ml / 4 2/3 tbs*
Raw papaya paste .... *60 gms / 4 tbs*
Red chilli powder .... *10 gms / 2 tsp*
Saffron (*kesar*) .... *2 gms*
Salt to taste
Vinegar .... *45 ml / 3 tbs*
Yoghurt, drained .... *200 gms / 1 cup*

Method:

1. Make a marinade with oil (4 tbs), vinegar, ginger and garlic pastes, salt, red chilli powder, black pepper and papaya.

2. Marinate the lamb in the paste for 2½ hours.

3. Mix together the yoghurt, oil (1 tbs) cheese, garam masala, cumin powder and saffron.

4. Add this to the lamb mixture and marinate it for 1 hour.

5. Thread the lamb pieces onto skewers, 3 cm apart.

6. Cook in a moderate tandoor/oven to 175 °C (350 °F) for 15 minutes or on a charcoal grill for 10-12 minutes.

7. Brush with butter and cook for another 3-4 minutes.

8. Remove from skewers and serve hot, on a bed of lettuce and green salad, accompanied by any Indian bread and Mint Chutney (page 10).

SEAFOOD

Crispy Sesame Prawns (recipe on following page) ▶

Crispy Sesame Prawns

Serves: 4   Preparation time: 2½ hours   Cooking time: 10-12 minutes

Ingredients:

Prawns (king size), shelled, deveined ..... *1 kg*
Oil for frying

For the first marinade:

Ginger paste (page 10) .... *20 gms / 4 tsp*
Garlic paste (page 10) .... *25 gms / 5 tsp*
White pepper powder .... *3 gms / ½ tsp*
Lemon juice .... *6 ml / 1 tsp*

For the second marinade:

Cheddar cheese, grated .... *60 gms / 4 tbs*

Carom (*ajwain*) seeds .... *15 gms / 1 tbs*
Cream .... *60 gms / 4 tbs*
Green cardamom (*choti elaichi*)
powder .... *3 gms / ½ tsp*
Mace (*javitri*) powder .... *3 gms / ½ tsp*
Gramflour (*besan*), roasted ..... *45 gms / 3 tbs*
Yoghurt, drained .... *120 gms / ½ cup*
Sesame (*til*) seeds .... *50 gms / ¼ cup*
Bread crumbs, powdered ..... *100 gms / 1 cup*

Method:

1. Mix all ingredients of first marinade, rub into the prawns. Keep aside for ½ hour.
2. Mix the ingredients for the second marinade (except sesame seeds and bread crumbs), marinate prawns in this for another ½ hour.
3. Combine bread crumbs and sesame seeds. Coat prawns with the mixture and chill for 15-20 minutes.
4. Heat oil in a *kadhai* (wok) till it is smoking, lower heat, fry prawns for 1-2 minutes. Drain, keep aside for 4-5 minutes. Deep fry again till they are crisp and golden in colour. Drain excess oil and serve hot, garnished with lemon wedges.

Garlic Prawn Kabab

Serves: 4   Preparation time: 2½ hours   Cooking time: 8-10 minutes

Ingredients:

Prawns (jumbo), shelled, deveined .... *1 kg*
Garlic paste (page 10) .... *15 gms / 1 tbs*
Green chilli paste (page 10) ..... *10 gms / 2 tsp*
Vinegar ....*30 ml / ¼ cup*

Salt to taste
Cornflour.................................... *15 gms / 1 tbs*
Butter for basting
Poppy (*khus khus*) seeds .... *15 gms / 1 tbs*

Method:

1. Marinate prawns in garlic-chilli pastes, vinegar and salt for 2 hours.
2. Mix in cornflour, skewer prawns 5 cms apart, roast on low flame, till crisp and golden on all sides, basting with butter. Coat with poppy seeds (optional) and serve hot.

◀ *Crispy Sesame Prawns (picture on preceding page)*

Tandoori Lobster

Serves: 4   Preparation time: 2 hours   Cooking time: 10-12 minutes

Ingredients:

Lobster (large) 2	Lemon juice .... *15 gms / 1 tbs*
Egg, whisked 1	Garam masala (page 10) .... *8 gms /1 ½ tsp*
Ginger, chopped .... *15 gms / 1 tbs*	White pepper, powdered............*3 gms / ½ tsp*
Cream ....*120 ml / ½ cup*	Carom (*ajwain*) seeds .... *7gms /1 ½ tsp*
Ginger paste (page 10) .... *15 gms / 1 tbs*	Gramflour (*besan*) .... *40 gms /2 ½ tbs*
Garlic paste (page 10) .... *15 gms / 1 tbs*	Salt to taste

Method:

1. Boil the lobsters and leave aside to cool.

2. Shell and devein the lobster, retaining the shell if it is to be used while serving.

3. To the egg, add ginger, cream, ginger garlic pastes, lemon juice, garam masala, white pepper, carom seeds, gramflour and salt. Whisk well.

4. Coat the lobsters with the prepared mixture and keep aside to marinate for 1½ hour.

5. Skewer each lobster separately.

6. Roast in a tandoor/oven/charcoal grill for 4-5 minutes. Hang skewers to allow excess liquids to drip, cook for 3-4 minutes, basting with butter/oil once.

7. Serve hot, accompanied by a green salad.

Pomegranate Prawns

Serves: 4   Preparation: 45 minutes   Cooking: 15 minutes

Ingredients:

Prawns (jumbo), shelled, deveined 8	Cheddar cheese, grated .... *30 gms / 2 tbs*
Malt vinegar ....*30 ml / 2 tbs*	Green coriander, chopped .... *10 gms / 2 tsp*
Salt to taste	Ginger, finely chopped .... *5 gms / 1 tsp*
Yellow chilli powder .... *2.5 gms / ½ tsp*	Cumin (*jeera*) seeds .... *2.5 gms / ½ tsp*
Ginger paste (page 10) .... *10 gms / 2 tsp*	Lemon juice ....*30 ml / 2 tbs*
Garlic paste (page 10) .... *10 gms / 2 tsp*	White pepper powder .... *2.5 gms / ½ tsp*
Peas, boiled and mashed ..... *120 gms / ½ cup*	Tomato ketchup ....*45 ml / 3 tbs*

Pomegranate seeds
(*anar dana*), fresh .... *240 gms / 1 cup*

Pickled onions, chopped .... *60 gms / ¼ cup*

Method:

1. Mix malt vinegar, salt, yellow chilli powder, ginger and garlic pastes and marinate prawns in it for half an hour.
2. Place each prawn on a 10" square piece of greased aluminium foil.
3. Mix cheese, onion, coriander, ginger, cumin, lemon juice, white pepper powder, tomato ketchup, peas and pomegranate seeds. Coat each prawn with this mixture.
4. Wrap up the foil and place the parcels in a baking tray, bake in a preheated oven at 275 °F for 10-12 minutes.

Prawn Cutlets

Serves: 4-6   Preparation time: 30 minutes   Cooking time: 30 minutes

Ingredients:

Prawns / Shrimps, shelled
and chopped .... *400 gms / 2 cups*
Onions (medium), finely chopped *2*
Ginger, chopped .... *15 gms / 1 tbs*
Green chillies, chopped *2*
Green coriander, chopped .... *15 gms / 1 tbs*
Salt to taste
Lemon juice .... *5 gms / 1 tsp*

Bread crumbs, dried, powdered
.... *200 gms / 1 cup*
Turmeric (*haldi*) powder .... *2 gms / ¼ tsp*
Black pepper powder .... *3 gms / ½ tsp*
Egg *1*
Bread crumbs, fresh .... *200 gms / 1 cup*
Oil for frying

Method:

1. Mix together, the prawns/shrimps, onions, ginger, chillies, coriander, salt, lemon juice, fresh bread crumbs, turmeric, black pepper and egg, knead well.
2. Divide mixture into eight portions and shape them into flat round cutlets.
3. Dip cutlets in dried bread crumbs, coating them evenly and brush off excess bread crumbs.
4. Heat oil in a *kadhai* (wok) till it is smoking. Lower cutlets gently into the oil and fry until they are golden brown, crisp and cooked through on each side.
5. Serve at once, accompanied by Mint Chutney (page 10).

Tandoori Prawns

Serves: 4   Preparation time: 2 hours   Cooking time: 15 minutes

Ingredients:

Prawns (king size) *12*
Ginger paste (page 10) .... *7 gms / 1 ½ tsp*
Garlic paste (page 10) .... *10 gms / 2 tsp*
Lemon juice .... *30 gms / 2 tbs*
Yoghurt .... *240 ml / 1 cup*
Gramflour (*besan*) .... *30 gms / 2 tbs*

Salt to taste
Carom (*ajwain*) seeds .... *5 gms /1 tsp*
Red chilli powder .... *5 gms / 1 tsp*
Garam masala (page 10) .... *5 gms / 1 tsp*
Turmeric (*haldi*) powder .... *3 gms / ½ tsp*

Method:

1. Combine ginger and garlic pastes alongwith lemon juice (1 tbs), rub into the prawns and put aside.

2. Whisk together yoghurt, gramflour, salt, carom seeds, chilli powder, garam masala and turmeric into a smooth paste. Marinate prawns in the paste for at least 2 hours.

3. Skewer the prawns gently and cook in a preheated (150 °C/300 °F) oven/tandoor/grill/ for about 12-15 minutes or till almost done.

4. Hang skewers for 3-5 minutes to allow the excess liquid to drip. Baste with oil and roast again for 3-5 minutes or till golden brown. Remove from skewers.

5. Sprinkle chaat masala and remaining lemon juice. Serve hot, accompanied by a salad.

Fish Kababs

Serves: 6   Preparation time: 1 hour   Cooking time: 30 minutes

Ingredients:

Fish fillets (3" × 2" × 1" pieces) .... *1 kg*
Onions, finely chopped .... *175 gms / ³/₅ cup*
Malt vinegar .... *45 ml / 3 tbs*
Green chillies,
finely chopped .... *25 gms / 5 tsp*
Green coriander, finely chopped ....
.... *15 gms / 1 tbs*

Ginger, finely chopped .... *15 gms*
Salt
Eggs *2*
Bread crumbs, powdered
Oil/Clarified butter (*ghee*) for frying

◀ *Tandoori Prawns*

Method:

1. Wash fish fillets and dry completely on paper napkin or cloth.
2. Soak chopped onions in vineger for an hour, so that it gets absorbed into the onions. Add chopped green chillies, coriander, ginger and salt, mix well.
3. In a seperate bowl, beat egg lightly and keep aside.
4. Apply the onion mixture thinly and evenly on both sides of each fish fillet, dip into beaten eggs and then coat well with bread crumbs. Press lightly on both sides to make the coating firm. Refrigerate fish fillets for half an hour to allow the coating to dry.
5. Heat oil in a pan and fry each kabab on meduim heat till crisp and golden brown. Serve hot, accompanied by Mint Chutney (page 10).

Tandoori Pomfret

Serves: 4   Preparation time: 3½ hours   Cooking time: 12-15 minutes

Ingredients:

Pomfret (450 gms each) 4	White pepper powder .... *5 gms / 1 tsp*
Yoghurt, drained .... *60 gms / 4 tbs*	Red chilli powder .... *10 gms / 2 tsp*
Eggs 2	Turmeric (*haldi*) powder .... *5 gms / 1 tsp*
Cream .... *45 ml / 3 tbs*	Cumin (*jeera*) powder .... *10 gms / 2 tsp*
Ginger paste (page 10) .... *17 gms / 3½ tsp*	Gramflour (*besan*) .... *30 gms / 2 tbs*
Garlic paste (page 10) .... *17 gms / 3½ tsp*	Lemon juice .... *30 gms / 2 tbs*
Carom (*ajwain*) seeds .... *10 gms / 2 tsp*	Butter/Oil for basting

Method:

1. Clean and wash the fish. Make 2-3 incisions on both sides.
2. Whisk together, the yoghurt and egg (yolks only) alongwith the remaining ingredients to make a smooth paste.
3. Evenly coat the fish with yoghurt paste and allow to marinate for atleast 3 hours.
4. Preheat oven to 175 °C / 350 °F.
5. Skewer the fish, from mouth to tail. Roast in tandoor, charcoal grill or oven for 10 minutes. Remove from heat and hang the skewers to let excess liquids drip. Baste with butter and roast again for 3-5 minutes.
6. Serve at once, accompanied by a salad.

◀ *Tandoori Pomfret*

Fish Tikka

Serves: 4-6   Preparation time: 1½ hours   Cooking time: 30 minutes

Ingredients:

Fish fillets, cut into cubes .... *1 kg*
Salt to taste
Lemon juice .... *15 gms / 1 tbs*
Yoghurt .... *120 gms / ³/₅ cup*
Vinegar .... *15 ml / 1 tbs*
Garam masala (page 10) .... *15 gms / 1 tbs*

Cumin (*jeera*) seeds, ground   *10 gms / 2 tsp*
Carom (*ajwain*) seeds .... *3 gms / ½ tsp*
Red chilli powder .... *5 gms / 1 tsp*
Garlic paste (page 10) .... *10 gms / 2 tsp*
Oil / Butter for basting

Method:

1. Wash and dry the cubed fish fillets. Sprinkle salt and lemon juice. Set aside to marinate for half an hour.

2. In a bowl, combine yoghurt with remaining ingredients and whisk well. Pour mixture over the fish cubes and coat evenly. Leave to marinate for at least one hour.

3. Preheat oven to 175 °C (350 °F).

4. Roast, bake or grill till the fillets are golden brown in colour and cooked through, basting just once.

5. Serve hot, accompanied by Mint Chutney (page 10).

Stuffed Tandoori Fish

Serves: 4-5   Preparation time: 3½ hours   Cooking time: 20 minutes

Ingredients:

River or sea fish
(with single centre bone), 400 gms each *5*
Salt to taste
Yoghurt, drained .... *200 gms / 1 cup*
Black pepper powder .... *10 gms / 2 tsp*
Fennel (*saunf*) seeds .... *10 gms / 2 tsp*
Garlic paste (page 10) .... *25 gms / 5 tsp*
Clarified butter (*ghee*) .... *50 ml / 3¹/₃ tbs*

Ginger paste (page 10) .... *25 gms / 5 tsp*
Gramflour (*besan*) .... *40 gms / 2²/₃ tbs*
Lemon juice .... *25 ml / 5 tsp*
Red chilli powder .... *20 gms / 4 tsp*
Turmeric (*haldi*) powder .... *10 gms / 2 tsp*
Malt vinegar .... *45 ml / 3 tbs*
Butter to baste .... *50 gms / 3¹/₃ tbs*

Method:

1. Marinate fish in vinegar and salt.

2. In a bowl, combine yoghurt alongwith black pepper powder, fennel seed, garlic paste, clarified butter, ginger paste, gramflour, lemon juice, red chilli powder, turmeric powder and mix to make a fine paste.

3. Marinate the fish in this paste and leave to stand for 2-3 hours.

4. Preheat the oven to 175 °C (350 °F).

5. Skewer the fish from mouth to tail, 4 cms apart. Roast in the oven for 12-15 minutes.

6. Baste with butter. Remove and hang the skewers to let the excess liquid drip.

7. Serve hot, garnished with slices of cucumber, tomato and onion rings and accompanied by Mint Chutney (page 10).

Fried Fish Patties

Serves: 4-6   Preparation time: 30 minutes   Cooking time: 30 minutes

Ingredients:

Fish fillets .... *250 gms*	Ginger, finely chopped .... *4 gms / ¾ tsp*
Salt to taste	Green coriander, chopped .... *15 gms / 1 tbs*
Bread crumbs, fresh .... *150 gms / ¾ cup*	Black pepper powder .... *3 gms / ½ tsp*
Onion (small), finely chopped *1*	Garam masala (page 10) .... *3 gms / ½ tsp*
Green chillies, finely chopped *2*	Oil for frying

Method:

1. Boil water with salt and lower fish fillets into the water. Allow to cook for 5-6 minutes.

2. Remove, drain excess water and put aside to cool.

3. Mash the fish, add all ingredients (except oil) and knead the mixture well.

4. Divide into equal sized portions and shape into flat round patties.

5. Heat oil in a *kadhai* (wok) till it is smoking. Slip in 4-5 fish patties at a time, fry till crisp and brown on both sides. Remove from oil and drain excess oil on a paper napkin.

6. Serve hot, garnished with chopped coriander and cream.

Fried Fish

Serves: 4-6   Preparation time: 1½ hours   Cooking time: 30 minutes

Ingredients:

Fish fillets 8
Salt to taste
Black pepper powder .... *5 gms / 1 tsp*
Lemon juice .... *15 gms / 1tbs*
Gramflour (*besan*) .... *75 gms / 5 tbs*
Rice flour.................................. *25 gms / 5 tsp*

Turmeric (*haldi*) powder .... *3 gms / ½ tsp*
Red chilli powder .... *5 gms / 1 tsp*
Water, cold................................. *100 ml / ½ cup*
Oil for deep frying
Chaat masala .... *a pinch*

Method:

1. Cut each fillet in half and sprinkle salt, pepper and lemon juice all over. Set aside to marinate for an hour.

2. Combine the gramflour, rice flour, turmeric powder and chilli powder in a bowl. Stir in the water to make a smooth batter. Dip each marinated fillet in batter to coat evenly and keep aside.

3. Heat oil in a *kadhai* (wok) till it is smoking. Carefully lower the fillet into the oil.

4. Fry until crisp and golden brown on both sides. Remove and drain excess oil.

5. Sprinkle chaat masala, garnish with lemon wedges and serve hot.

Fish Fillets in a Spiced Marinade

Serves: 4-5   Preparation time: 2-4 hours   Cooking time: 15 minutes

Ingredients:

Fish fillets ....*1 kg*
Salt to taste
Vinegar.....................................*50 ml / ¼ cup*
Carom (*ajwain*) seeds .... *10 gms / 2 tsp*
White pepper powder .... *8 gms / 1⅔ tsp*
Turmeric (*haldi*) powder .... *8 gms / 1⅔ tsp*
Red chilli powder .... *8 gms / 1⅔ tsp*

Gramflour (*besan*) .... *120 gms / ⅔ cup*
Ginger paste (page 10) .... *60 gms / 4 tbs*
Garlic paste (page 10) .... *60 gms / 4 tbs*
Lemon juice .... *50 ml / 4 tbs*
Oil ....*200 ml / 1 cup*
Chaat masala .... *6 gms / 1 tsp*

◀ *Fried Fish*

Method:

1. Clean, wash and dry the fish.

2. Prick each piece of fish with a sharp fork.

3. Marinate the fish fillets with salt and two-thirds of vinegar, let them stand for 1-2 hours.

4. In a bowl, combine the carom seeds, white pepper powder, turmeric, red chilli, gramflour alongwith the ginger and garlic pastes, lemon juice, the remaining vinegar and salt. Whisk to a smooth and creamy batter.

5. Coat each piece of fish evenly with the prepared batter.

6. Arrange the fillets on a flat tray and keep aside for 1-2 hours at room temperature.

7. Heat oil in a heavy bottomed pan over medium heat. Shallow fry the fish till crisp and golden on both sides.

8. Drain excess oil on kitchen towels and sprinkle chaat masala.

9. Serve hot, garnished by slices of cucumber, tomato and lemon wedges, accompanied by Mint Chutney (page 10).

Shredded Stir-Fried Pomfret

Serves: 4-6   Preparation time: 20 minutes   Cooking time: 25 minutes

Ingredients:

Pomfrets (medium sized), shredded 2
Ginger paste (page 10) .... *5 gms /1 tsp*
Garlic paste (page 10) .... *5 gms / 1 tsp*
Onions (medium), finely chopped 2
Green chillies, sliced 4
Coconut (fresh), grated .... *400 gms / 2 cups*

Green coriander, chopped .... *30 gms / 2 tbs*
Turmeric (*haldi*) powder .... *5 gms / 1 tsp*
Lemon juice .... *15 gms / 1 tbs*
Salt to taste
Oil for frying .... *60 ml / 4 tbs*
Vinegar .... *15 gms / 1 tbs*

Method:

1. Heat oil in a pan, add ginger and garlic pastes, sauté till brown.

2. Add onions and green chillies. Fry till golden brown.

3. Add coconut, coriander, turmeric powder, lemon juice and salt. Cook on slow fire for 5 minutes.

4. Add fish and stir gently till the fish is done. Serve hot, accompanied by any Indian bread.

VEGETABLES

Potato Baskets (recipe on following page) ▶

Potato Baskets

Serves: 4-6   Preparation time: 5-6 minutes

Ingredients:

Potatoes (large), boiled and peeled 8
Chickpeas (*kabuli chana*),
boiled .... *150 gms / ¾ cup*
Chaat masala .... *15 gms / 1 tbs*
Ginger, finely chopped .... *15 gms / 1 tbs*

Green chillies, finely chopped *10 gms / 2 tsp*
Green coriander, finely chopped ....
.... *15 gms / 1 tbs*
Lemon juice .... *30 ml / 2 tbs*
Salt to taste

Method:

1. Cut potatoes in half and carefully scoop out the centres.
2. Mix together chickpeas, chaat masala, ginger, green chillies, coriander, lemon juice and salt, fill it in the centre of scooped potatoes. Serve on a flat dish.

Vegetable Pappad Rolls

Serves: 4   Preparation time: 20 minutes   Cooking time: 5 minutes

Ingredients:

*Pappad, medium sized *4*
Carrot (medium sized), chopped *1*
Potato (medium sized), chopped *1*
French beans, chopped *6*
Cauliflower, chopped .... *100 gms / ½ cup*
Salt to taste

Tomato, chopped *1*
Oil for frying
Turmeric (*haldi*) powder .... *½ tsp*
Red chilli powder .... *½ tsp*
Green coriander, chopped .... *15 gms / 1 tbs*

Method:

*   Lentil based wafer-thin snack, eaten roasted or fried — easily available at any Indian food store.
1. Boil the chopped carrot, potato, french beans and cauliflower with a pinch of salt till almost cooked. Drain water and allow vegetables to dry out.
2. Stir- fry the tomatoes in oil (1 tbs). Add boiled vegetables, alongwith turmeric and chilli powder. Stir and add coriander. Remove from heat and allow cool.
3. Take a *pappad,* dip it in water (to make it pliable), put a little vegetable mixture along the centre and fold both sides over. Press each end well to seal.
4. Heat oil till it is smoking. Deep fry *pappad* rolls on each side till crisp. Remove and serve immediately..

◀ *Potato Baskets (picture on preceding page)*

Semolina Fritters

Serves: 4-6   Preparation time: 25 minutes   Cooking time: 10 minutes

Ingredients:

Semolina (*sooji*) .... *150 gms / 1½ cups*
Yoghurt .... *120 gms / 1 cup*
Water .... *120 ml / 8 tbs*
Onions (small), chopped *2*
Green chillies, finely chopped *2*

Green coriander, chopped .... *15 gms / 1 tbs*
Salt
Asafoetida (*heeng*) .... *a pinch (optional)*
Oil for frying
Peas (semi-boiled) .... *½ cup*

Method:

1. Sieve semolina in a large bowl. Add yoghurt and water, mix well and set aside for 20-30 minutes.
2. Add onions, green chillies, coriander, salt, peas, asafoetida and a little oil to the semolina mixture and mix well.
3. Heat oil in a *kadhai*(wok) till it is smoking.
4. Drop spoonfulls of batter into the oil, do not let them stick together and deep fry until crisp and brown. Serve hot, accompanied by Mint or Coconut Chutney (page 10).

Corn Croquettes

Serves: 2-3   Preparation time: 15 minutes   Cooking time: 5-10 minutes

Ingredients:

Corn (fresh), grated .... *200 gms / 1 cup*
Bread slices *2*
Ginger paste (page 10) .... *5 gms / 1 tsp*
Green chilli paste (page 10) .... *5 gms / 1 tsp*

White pepper powder .... *3 gms / ½ tsp*
Green coriander, chopped .... *15 gms / 1 tbs*
Salt to taste

Method:

1. Combine all the ingredients and mix well.
2. Divide mixture into lemon sized balls. Flatten each ball into a round patty.
3. Heat oil till smoking and shallow fry till golden brown on each side.
4. Serve hot, accompanied by Mint Chutney (page 10)

Crispy Lentil Strips

Serves: 4-6   Preparation time: 5-6 hours   Cooking time: 30 minutes

Ingredients:

Lentils (*chana daal*) .... 200 gms
Coriander seeds .... 15 gms / 1 tbs
Peppercorns .... 15 gms / 1 tbs
Ginger, chopped .... 10 gms / 2 tsp
Green coriander, chopped .... 15 gms /1 tbs

Green chillies, chopped 2
Salt to taste
Red chilli powder .... 5 gms / 1 tsp
Garam masala (page 10) .... 5 gms / 1 tsp
Oil for frying

Method:

1. Soak lentils for 4-5 hours or in warm water for ½ hour. Drain and blend alongwith coriander seeds and pepper corns to make a coarsely ground thick paste.
2. Put the paste into a big bowl and add the remaining ingredients, mix thoroughly and keep aside for 30 minutes.
3. Heat oil in a *kadhai* (wok) till it is smoking. Moisten hands and shape the mixture into 10 cm flat patties. Fry patties for 2-3 minutes on both sides and remove from oil. Drain excess oil and allow to cool.
4. Slice the patties into 3-4 strips. Reheat oil till smoking, lower heat to medium and fry the strips till they are crisp and golden brown on both sides. Drain excess oil and serve hot, accompanied by Mint Chutney (page 10).

Lentil Croquettes

Serves: 4   Preparation: 30 minutes   Cooking: 10 minutes

Ingredients:

Lentils (*gram daal*) .... 300 gms / 1½ cups
Cumin (*jeera*) seeds .... 5 gms / 1 tsp
Onions, chopped .... 60 gms / ½ cups
Ginger, chopped .... 30 gms / 2 tbs

Green coriander, chopped .... 20 gms / 1 tbs
Green chillies, chopped 5
Salt to taste
Oil for frying

Method:

1. Soak lentils for 6 hours. Drain and grind coarsely alongwith cumin seeds.
2. Add onions, ginger, coriander, green chillies and salt. Mix well, divide into equal sized portions, shape into round croquettes/cutlets. Deep fry in hot oil till crisp and golden brown. Serve hot, accompanied by Coconut Chutney (page 10).

◀ *Crispy Lentil Strips*

Stuffed Tomatoes

Serve: 4-5   Preparation time: 30 minutes   Cooking time:10 minutes

Ingredients:

Tomatoes (large) 6
Spring onions, chopped .... *60 gms / 4 tbs*
Butter .... *15 gms / 1 tbs*
Mushrooms , chopped .... *200 gms / 1 cup*
Cream .... *15 gms / 1 tbs*
Salt to taste
Green coriander, chopped .... *15 gms / 1 tbs*
White pepper .... *5 gms / 1 tsp*

Method:

1. Slice each tomato at the top. Scoop out seeds and keep the tomato cup and top aside.
2. Sauté spring onions for two minutes in butter. Add mushrooms, cream, salt, coriander and pepper, sauté for 5 minutes. Remove and keep aside.
3. Drain excess moisture from mushrooms, carefully fill each tomato cup with the mushroom mixture. Cover with the top and secure with tooth-picks.
4. Preheat oven to 150 °C / (300 °F). Place stuffed tomatoes on a baking tray and bake for 8-10 minutes. Remove tooth-picks and serve hot.

Stir-Fried Whole Peas

Serves: 4-6   Preparation time: 20 minutes   Cooking time: 10 minutes

Ingredients:

Peas, unshelled .... *½ kg*
Oil .... *15 ml / 1 tbs*
Asafoetida (*heeng*) powder .... *a pinch*
Green chillies, chopped *2*
Raw mango powder (*amchoor*) *5 gms / 1 tsp*
Red chilli powder .... *3 gms / ½ tsp*
Salt
Garam masala (page 10) .... *5 gms / 1 tsp*

Method:

1. Wash whole green peas and pat dry.
2. Heat oil in a deep pan, add asafoetida. Cook for 1 minute then mix in green chillies and green peas. Cover the pan and let peas cook on low heat for at least 8-10 minutes, or until they are almost cooked.
3. Add mango powder, red chilli, salt and garam masala. Stir and continue to cook for 3-4 minutes. Remove from fire, put on a flat serving dish, and serve very hot.

◀ *Stuffed Tomatoes*

Stuffed Capsicums

Serves: 4-5   Preparation time: 30 minutes   Cooking time: 10 minutes

Ingredients:

Capsicum (large) 6
Butter/Oil for cooking .... *15 gms / 1 tbs*
Spring onions .... *120 gms / 1 cup*
Green coriander, chopped .... *15 gms / 1 tbs*
Cottage cheese, (*paneer*) grated
.... *250 gms / 2¼ cups*

Salt to taste
Chaat masala .... *15 gms / 1 tbs*
Green chillies, chopped 4
Cumin (*jeera*) powder .... *10 gms / 2 tsp*

Method:

* For recipe of *paneer*, turn to page 10.

1. Slice each capsicum from the top. Scoop out seeds and keep capsicum cup and top aside.
2. Heat butter/oil in a pan. Stir-fry spring onions, add coriander, cottage cheese, salt, chaat masala, green chillies and cumin powder. Cook further for 4-5 minutes. Remove from heat.
3. Fill the cottage cheese mixture into the capsicum cups and cover the top with the capsicum slice. Secure with tooth-picks.
4. Preheat oven to 150 °C / (300 °F). Place stuffed capsicums on a baking tray or skewer carefully and grill on charcoal for 8-10 minutes till the skin of capsicum develops golden brown spots. Remove tooth-picks and serve hot.

Grilled Cottage Cheese Rolls

Serves: 4   Preparation: 10 minutes   Cooking: 20 minutes

Ingredients:

Cottage cheese (*paneer*),
in a firm block, ... 500 gms
—grated (for stuffing) .... *150 gms / ¾ cup*
For the stuffing:
Oil .... *75 ml / 5 tbs*
Mushrooms, chopped .... *150 gms / ¾ cup*
Capsicum, chopped .... *150 gms / ¾ cup*
Onions, chopped .... *150 gms / ¾ cup*

Coconut powder .... *100 gms / ½ cup*
Cayenne pepper .... *10 gms / 2 tsp*
Black cumin (*shah jeera*) .... *5 gms / 1 tsp*
Fenugreek (*kasoori methi*) powder
.... *5 gms / 1 tsp*
Salt to taste
Lemon juice .... *10 ml / 2 tsp*
Potatoes, boiled and grated *100 gms / ½ cup*

◀ *Stuffed Capsicum*

Raisins .... 100 gms / ½ cup	Gramflour (*besan*) .... 50 gms / ¼ cup
Turmeric (*haldi*) powder .... 5 gms / 1 tsp	Cream .... 100 ml / ½ cup
White pepper powder .... 20 gms / 4 tsp	Green coriander, chopped .... 20 gms / 4 tsp
For the coating:	Saffron (*kesar*) .... 0.5 gms
Cornflour .... 100 gms / ½ cup	Water .... 20 ml / 4 tsp

Method:

1. Slice cottage cheese lengthwise into 15 × 6 × 0.5 cm pieces.
2. Heat oil, sauté mushrooms, capsicum, onion and coconut powder. Add cottage cheese alongwith other ingredients for the filling. Stir-fry for a few seconds and remove from heat.
3. Mix gramflour with just enough water to make a thick paste. Spread the paste on one side of each cottage cheese slice, turn over, spread 3 tsp of the filling and roll into a cylindrical shape. Similarly, prepare other rolls and keep aside.
4. To the gramflour-water paste, add the remaining ingredients for the coating. Coat each stuffed cottage cheese roll evenly and bake in a oven for 10-12 minutes at low heat.
5. Sprinkle with chaat masala, serve hot, garnished with grated carrots and lemon wedges.

Cottage Cheese Seekh Kabab

Serves: 4-5   Preparation time: 15 minutes   Cooking time: 15 minutes

Ingredients:

Cottage cheese (**paneer*), grated .... 1 kg	Cumin (*jeera*) powder .... 5 gms / 1 tsp
Green chillies, chopped .... 30 gms / 2 tbs	Red chilli powder .... 5 gms / 1 tsp
Onions, grated 2	Salt to taste
Ginger, coarsely ground .... 15 gms / 1 tbs	Butter for basting
Green coriander, chopped .... 30 gms / 2 tbs	Cornflour .... 20 gms / 4 tsp
Black pepper .... 10 gms / 2 tsp	

Method:

* For recipe of *paneer*, turn to page 10

1. Mix all the ingredients, adding the cornflour in the end and knead well.
2. Moisten hands and wrap the cottage cheese mixture around the skewers to form a kabab 4-5" long and 2" apart.
3. Roast in a preheated (150 °C / 300 °F) oven/tandoor/charcoal grill for 5-6 minutes, basting occasionally with melted butter.
4. Serve hot, accompanied by salad and/or Mint Chutney (page 10).

◀ *Cottage Cheese Seekh Kabab*

Cottage Cheese Croquettes

Serves: 4   Preparation time: 10 minutes   Cooking time:15 minutes

Ingredients:

Cottage cheese (*paneer*), grated .... *500 gms*
Green chillies, chopped *4*
Green coriander, chopped .... *15 gms / 1 tbs*
White pepper .... *5 gms / 1 tsp*
Red chilli powder .... *5 gms / 1 tsp*

Carom (*ajwain*) seeds .... *3 gms / ½ tsp*
Egg (optional) *1*
Garam masala (page 10) .... *5 gms / 1 tsp*
Oil for frying
Gramflour (*besan*) .... *75 gms / ¾ cup*

Method:

* For recipe of *paneer*, turn to page 10.

1. Combine grated cottage cheese and all other ingredients adding gramflour in the end and mix together in a bowl to make a smooth paste.

2. Shape the mixture into round croquettes/cutlets.

3. Heat oil in a *kadhai* (wok) till it is smoking. Slide in a few cutlets/croquettes at a time into the oil and fry till they are golden brown and crisp on all sides.

4. Serve hot, accompanied by Mint Chutney (page 10).

Mushroom Cutlets

Serves: 3-4   Preparation time: 30-40 minutes   Cooking time: 15-20 minutes

Ingredients:

Mushrooms, chopped .... *150 gms*
Potatoes, boiled and skinned *3*
Peas, boiled .... *50 gms / ½ cup*
Onions (medium), finely chopped *3*
Green chillies, finely chopped *3*
Ginger, finely chopped .... *5gms / 1tsp*

Coconut, fresh grated.................. *15gms / 1tbs*
Red chilli powder ....*5gm / 1tsp*
Turmeric (*haldi*) powder .... *3gms / ½ tsp*
Green coriander, chopped .... *15gms / 1tbs*
Bread crumbs, pounded.............. *3gms / 2tbs*
Gramflour (*besan*) .... *100 gms / 1cup*

Method:

1. Combine chopped mushrooms, potatoes and peas together.

2. Add chopped onions, green chillies, ginger, grated coconut, red chilli powder, turmeric powder and coriander, mix well. Season with salt. Mix the coarsely pounded breadcrumbs.

◀ *Cottage Cheese Croquettes*

3. **For the batter**, take gramflour in a large bowl, add water and a pinch of salt to make a batter of coating consistency, mix thoroughly.

4. Take the mushroom mixture, shape into flat round cutlets.

5. Heat oil in a frying pan till it is smoking. Dip each cutlet lightly in the gram flour batter and fry till each side is crisp and golden brown.

6. Serve hot, accompanied by Mint Chutney (page 10).

Cheesy Tandoori Mushrooms

Serves: 4   Preparation time: 45 minutes   Cooking time: 20 minutes

Ingredients:

Mushrooms	*200 gms*	Coriander powder	*3 gms/½ tsp*
Tomato sauce	*90 gms / 6 tbs*	Garam masala (page 10)	*3 gms / ½ tsp*
Ginger paste (page 10)	*15 gms / 1tbs*	Red colour,	*a pinch*
Garlic paste (page 10)	*15 gms / 1 tbs*	Cream	*75 ml / ¾ cup*
Red chilli powder	*5 gms / 1 tsp*	Cheese, grated	*1 cup*
Turmeric (*haldi*) powder	*3 gms / ½ tsp*	Green coriander, chopped	*15 gms / 1tbs*
Cumin (*jeera*) powder	*3 gms / ½ tsp*		

Method:

1. Mix the tomato sauce with ginger/garlic paste. Add all the spices and salt. Marinate the mushrooms in this mixture for 15 minutes. Mix in cream.

2. Grease a baking dish, pour the mushrooms along with the creamy marinade into it. Top with grated cheese and bake in a preheated oven for 20 minutes. Serve hot, garnished with chopped coriander and accompanied by Mint Chutney (page 10).

ACCOMPANIMENTS & DESSERTS

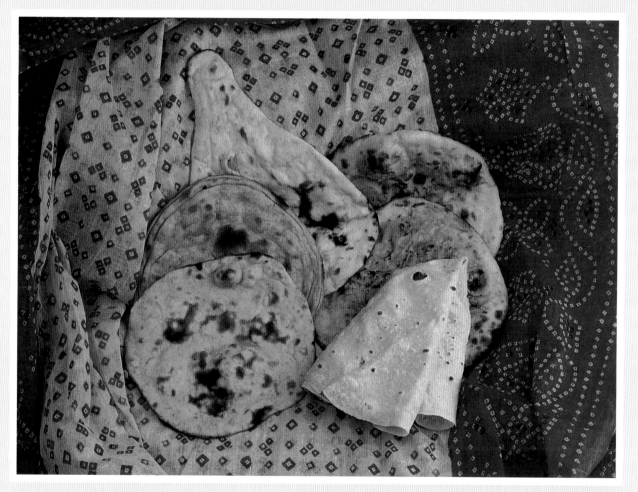

Assorted Indian Breads (recipes on following pages) ▶

Naan

Serves: 4-5   Preparation time: 3 hours   Cooking time: 20 min

Ingredients:

Flour .... *500 gms / 2½ cups*
Baking powder .... *5 gms / 1 tsp*
Baking soda .... *1 gm / ¼ tsp*
Clarified butter (ghee)/Oil .... *25 ml / 5 tsp*
Egg *1*

Melon (*magaz*) seeds .... *5 gms / 1 tsp*
Milk .... *50 ml / 3⅓ tbs*
Onion (*kalonji*) seeds .... *3 gms / ⅔ tsp*
Salt to taste
Sugar .... *10 gms / 2 tsp*

Method:

1. Sieve the flour, salt, baking soda and baking powder into a bowl. Add enough water to make a hard dough.
2. Whisk egg, sugar and milk in a bowl and knead into the dough to make it soft and smooth. Cover with moist cloth, keep aside for 10 minutes.
3. Add oil, knead and punch the dough, cover again with moist cloth, keep aside for 2 hours to allow the dough to rise.
4. Heat the oven till moderately hot—175°C (350 °F).
5. Divide the dough into 6 balls and place on a lightly floured surface. Sprinkle onion and melon seeds, flatten the balls slightly, cover and keep aside for 5 minutes.
6. Flatten each ball between the palms to make a round disc, then stretch on one side to form an elongated oval.
7. Place on a greased baking tray and bake for 2-3 min.
8. Serve hot, as an accompaniment to any curry dish.

Masala Poori

Serves: 16   Preparation time: 3 hours   Cooking time: ½ hour

Ingredients:

Flour, sieved .... *400 gms / 2 cups*
Salt .... *2 gms / ½ tsp*
Cayenne pepper or paprika ..... *1 gm / a pinch*
Turmeric (*haldi*) powder .... *1 gm / a pinch*
Coriander, ground .... *10 gms / 2 tsp*

Cumin (*jeera*), ground .... *7 gms / 1⅔ tsp*
Oil or Butter, melted .... *30 gms /2 tbs*
Water, warm .... *160 ml / ¾ cup*
Oil for frying

◀ *Naan (picture on preceding page)*

Method:

1. Mix the flour, salt, cayenne pepper, turmeric, coriander and cumin. Add oil/butter and rub it in till it is thoroughly incorporated. Add water, knead into a medium soft dough.
2. Lightly oil your palms and knead until the dough is silky smooth and pliable. Shape into a smooth ball. Brush with oil and keep aside for 3 hours.
3. Knead again briefly, divide into 16 equal portions and shape into balls.
4. Compress each into a 2" patty. Dip one end of the patty in oil and roll out into a 5" round, place on a flat surface. Similarly, roll out the other portions.
5. Heat oil in a *kadhai* (wok). Carefully slip one round into the hot oil. Fry until it puffs up and is golden brown on both sides. Remove and drain on paper towels.
6. Serve hot as an accompaniment to any curry dish.

Lachha Parantha

Serves: 4   Preparation time: 1½ hrs   Cooking time: 30 minutes

Ingredients:

Flour .... *480 gms / 2 ¹/₃ cups*
Fennel (*saunf*) .... *10 gms / 2 tsp*
Clarified butter (*ghee*) .... *180 ml / ¾ cup*
Clarified butter to shallow fry

Milk ....*240 ml / 1¼ cup*
Salt to taste
Water .... *120 ml / ²/₃ cup*

Method:

1. Pound fennel with a pestle.
2. Sieve flour and salt together. Make a well in the flour and pour in milk and water. Mix gradually and knead into a dough. Cover with moist cloth and keep aside for 10 min.
3. Melt ¹/₃ of the clarified butter, add to the dough, kneading constantly to make it soft and smooth.
4. Add pounded fennel and knead again for 5 minutes.
5. Divide into 12 equal balls, dust lightly, roll into 6" discs. Apply clarified butter 1 tsp evenly over one side.
6. Make a radial cut and fold disc into a narrow conical shape. Place flat side of the cone on palm and twist palms together in a round movement to compress dough into a thick flat round (*pedha*). Dust with flour, roll it out into an 8 inch disc. Refrigerate for an hour on butter paper.
7. Heat griddle and shallow fry both sides over low heat till golden.
8. Serve hot, accompanied by Raita (page 81) or any curry dish.

◀ *Lachha Parantha (picture on page 77)*

Mint Raita

Serves: 4   Preparation time: 10 minutes

Ingredients:

Yoghurt .... *600 ml / 3 cups*   Cumin (*jeera*) powder .... *2.5 gms / ½ tsp*
Mint leaves, dried, crushed ...... *75 gms / 5 tbs*

Method:

1. In a bowl, whisk yoghurt alongwith salt and cumin powder.

2. Add the mint leaves.

3. Refrigerate for half an hour.

4. Sprinkle mint leaves (1 tbs) and serve as an accompaniment to any dish.

Mixed Vegetable Raita

Serves: 4   Preparation time: 20 minutes

Ingredients:

Yoghurt .... *600 ml / 3 cups*   crushed .... *5 gms / 1 tsp*
Black peppercorns, roasted,   Cucumber, chopped .... *30 gms / 2 tbs*
crushed .... *2.5 gms / ½ tsp*   Green chilli, finely chopped .... *5 gms / 1 tsp*
Coriander seeds, roasted,   Onions, chopped .... *30 gms / 2 tbs*
crushed .... *5 gms / 1 tsp*   Tomatoes, chopped .... *30 gms / 2 tbs*
Cumin (*jeera*) seeds, roasted,

Method:

1. Whisk yoghurt alongwith salt in a bowl.

2. Add the chopped onions, tomatoes, cucumber and green chillies. Mix well.

3. Refrigerate for half an hour.

4. Sprinkle the crushed spices and serve as an accompaniment to any dish.

◀ *Mint Raita*

Rajbhog

Serves:8   Preparation time: 30 minutes   Cooking time: 3-4 hours

Ingredients:

For the filling:

Whole milk .... *320 ml*
Sugar .... *30 gms / 2 tbs*
Pistachios, grated .... *45 gms / 3 tbs*
Green cardamoms(*choti elaichi*),crushed *5*
For the *chenna* dumplings:
Whole milk ....*2 litres*

Lemon juice, strained .... *60 ml / 4 tbs*
Water ....*2 litres*
Sugar ....*1.5 kg*
Cornstarch (dissolved in 2tbs water) ....
.... *15 gms /1tbs*
Rose essence .... *¹/₃ tsp*

Method:

1. **For the filling**, boil milk and sugar in a heavy bottomed pan, till the quantity reduces to half a cup. Reduce heat, add nuts and cardamom, cook until the mixture pulls away from the sides of the pan, scrape the paste into a plate and set aside to cool.

2. **For the *chenna* dumplings**, heat milk over high heat, bring to a frothing boil, stirring constantly. Reduce heat, add lemon juice to make the milk curdle and the cheese to separate from the whey. If it does not, then add another tbs of lemon juice. Remove from heat and set aside to cool.

3. Pour the cheese-whey mixture into a moist cheese cloth. Gather the 4 corners of the cloth and rinse under tap water for 10 minutes. Gently twist the cloth to squeeze out excess water. Tie the corners and hang for 20-45 minutes to allow to drain.

4. Meanwhile, boil water and sugar in a pan, stirring continuously until sugar dissolves completely. Increase heat, cook for another 5 minutes. Remove from heat and set aside.

5. Unwrap the cheese on a clean work surface, crumble it repeatedly till it becomes fluffy and even. Divide into 8 balls and flatten into patties, 1 ¼" in diameter. Divide the filling in 8 portions, place one in the centre of each patty and roll to form seamless balls.

6. Reheat sugar syrup, bring to a boil and slide in the prepared balls. Increase heat and boil continuously for about 20 minutes, adding cornstarch with ¼ cup water after 4 minutes of boiling. Thereafter, ¼ cup water after every 4 minutes to maintain the consistency of the syrup. Take care to add water directly into the syrup and not on the balls. Remove from heat.

7. Allow to cool for 10 minutes, sprinkle the rose essence. Leave to soak the dumplings at room temperature for atleast 4 hours before consumption. Serve chilled or at room temperature.

◀ *Rajbhog*

INDEX